THE TOWN BEAR

CAROL J. COOPER

Archway Publishing books may be ordered through booksellers or by contacting:

Archway Publishing
1663 Liberty Drive
Bloomington, IN 47403
www.archwaypublishing.com
844-669-3957

ISBN: 978-1-6657-4331-0 (sc)
ISBN: 978-1-6657-4329-7 (hc)
ISBN: 978-1-6657-4330-3 (e)

Print information available on the last page.

Archway Publishing rev. date: 06/12/2023

Dedication

This book is dedicated to my grandson, Orion. May he always have a special kind of love for all living creatures, and hold bears in high esteem and honor.

Acknowledgments

With tremendous gratitude, I would like to thank Deputies Curt Dobbs and Winston Collins, as well as Jerry Kiger from the Missouri State Conservation Department, for their quick response, amazing help, and tremendous compassion that they shared on the day the bear showed up in my garage. You guys were AWESOME!

I would like to thank Manuel Hambelton for his consent in the use of the photo that he took of the bear attempting to climb back up the rock cliff, after being chased off by the pack of dogs.

A huge thank you goes out to Kenna Kenworthy for her editorial skills, support, and encouragement with this project.

Finally, a heartfelt thank you to my family and friends who knew how much this bear touched my heart and strongly encouraged me to put into writing what a meaningful moment this experience was.

The Town Bear

Life for this tiny little black bear began as it had for many generations before him, in the beautiful rolling hills and forests of the Ozarks. His mother **(sow)** made a safe, cozy den in the rocky cavities and gave birth to three tiny cubs in the cold month of January.

While she slept peacefully (**torpor**) during the long winter months, the mother bear would occasionally awaken to leave her den in search of food on mild winter days, always returning to her place of refuge and the three petite cubs. Being an **omnivore**, which means she ate both plants and animals, her search may have included many types of plants, grasses, berries, nuts, acorns, bees, ants, and small animals. She used her keen senses of smell and hearing to help guide her in the quest for food.

Cubs are very small at birth, and this little bear cub only weighed 10 ounces when he entered this world. He was born blind and covered in fine hair. Nourished by his mother's warm milk, he and his siblings began to grow very quickly. He would stay with his mother over the next year and a half before becoming a **yearling**.

His protective mother taught him the many skills he needed to survive, such as what foods to eat and where to find them. When danger approached, she taught the cubs how to use their strong paws and claws to grip and climb the trees to escape an encounter. He needed many lessons over time to prepare him for eventually leaving the family unit in search of his own area to live, his **home range**.

He became a fast runner, at times up to 30 miles an hour. He also became a very good swimmer and would hunt for fish in the crystal clear, cold creeks and lakes. He would splash in the water as he turned over the rocks in search of the elusive crayfish that lived below them.

You would think that all black bears have dark, shaggy, thick black fur; but this little fellow was more of a light cinnamon color, with a darker face and paws. Some black bears can have white spots on them; and in very rare cases can be almost completely white.

Normally, wild bears can live up to over 20 years deep within the woods and forests, far away from humans and civilization. Sadly, this would not be the case with our special bear. For whatever reason, this young bear had ventured close to a town in his search to find his own home range.

Perhaps it was the tempting odors he could smell across the winds when he stood upright on his rear legs. Perhaps it was easier to travel over the flatter and simpler layout of the land while he explored, versus the steep hills and cliffs of the mountains. Could it have been the voices of distant ancestors calling him to this place? Whatever it was that drew him there, he soon found himself in the confusion and busy world of a small rural town on the southern border of Missouri.

This town had a total population of only 773 people, and their homes and cattle farms were scattered and spread across the scenic land. Neighbors were often separated by many miles. Almost everyone had dogs and cats as pets in their home, living in their barn, or as working animals on their farm.

It was mid-May, unusually hot and humid for this time of the year for both humans and animals. The bear had wandered dangerously close to several homes situated on a high, rocky bluff.

When he got too close to one home, several of the family's dogs took chase after him. His heart pounded in fear as he turned and ran as fast as he could in the opposite direction of the fast approaching, aggressive pack of dogs. In his fright and confusion, he ran right off a cliff and fell 30 feet down onto the rocky ground along the highway.

His fall kept the dogs from attacking him, but also left him severely injured and in great pain. While the dogs viciously barked above him, he lay on the ground and tried to catch his breath and gather what strength he had. People who had witnessed his fall began pulling their vehicles over to see what would happen next.

Some folks who had lived here all their lives had never even seen a wild bear, and here was one right before their eyes! Several people took pictures as the injured bear rose from the rocks and crossed the highway. He tried his very best to crawl up the steep rocky hillside to the safety above him.

His picture appeared in the local town newspaper that week. It showed how frightened and injured he was as he found a way back up the rock bluffs. People saw him limp off into the thick woods; but for an entire week, no one actually knew of the young bear's whereabouts. Perhaps he just lay exhausted in pain, hunger, and thirst, too weak to get up and move.

A week later, a lady, who lived along that same bluff, went outside and opened her overhead garage door. Her dog, an Australian Shepherd, was by her side and began acting very strangely. The dog took a few steps, her nose in the air sniffing, and sensed that something very different was nearby.

The woman returned to her house for a short time before once again going outside. As she stood on her driveway, she heard things falling and breaking in one corner of the garage. She thought it must be one of the pesky raccoons that visited her home on a regular basis in search of food and tidbits. You can imagine her shock when she realized that it actually was a bear! Not only was it a bear, but she soon recognized that this was indeed "The Town Bear" she had seen in the newspaper.

She quickly closed the garage door to keep the bear contained inside. After several phone calls, a county deputy and an agent from the Missouri State Conservation Department soon arrived to see what they could do to help with the situation. The young bear was never aggressive with the people who watched him in wonder. He was a bear with a gentle soul.

It soon became very apparent that this young bear had sought a safe, quiet place where he could rest and take his very last breath in peace. He had chosen this woman's garage to be his **den**, his final "safe haven." Within a few hours, his struggle was over.

Over the next couple days, that beautiful creature became "famous" with his picture in the paper; and a television reporter even came out to interview the woman about the amazing experience that had not only touched her life, but the lives of so many in that small town. His story was soon seen by thousands of people, all moved by the young bear's appearance, gentle nature, and epic battle to survive.

NEWS

Was it a mere coincidence that the woman blessed with his arrival had many bear artifacts, pictures, and sculptures of black bears throughout her home long before this bear appeared? She had always felt a very strong kinship to nature's creatures, especially bears and wolves, and felt they were spirit animals that help guide us through our journey here on Earth.

Bless our Cabin
WELCOM

The gentleness of this young animal, despite his pain and suffering, spoke to her heart deeply, and she would forever be grateful for the incredible gift of this remarkable encounter. The spirit of this special bear continues to live on with those he touched on that special day.

A bystander stopped their car and took this photo of the bear after it had fallen off the rock bluff, and was attempting to climb back up.

A photo of the actual bear that the author found in her garage.

<u>Glossary</u>

Den - a cave or hole bears dig in the ground to use for hibernating

Home Range - the area of land that a bear takes as its territory to live in

Omnivore - an animal that eats both plants and meat

Sow - a mother bear

Torpor - the word for when bears hibernate during the cold, winter months

Yearling - a bear that is one year old